FLUTE

101 HIT SONGS

Available for
FLUTE, CLARINET, ALTO SAX, TENOR SAX, TRUMPET,
HORN, TROMBONE, VIOLIN, VIOLA, CELLO

ISBN 978-1-4950-7343-4

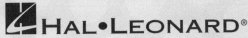

HAL•LEONARD®

7777 W. BLUEMOUND RD. P.O. BOX 13819 MILWAUKEE, WI 53213

Visit Hal Leonard Online at
www.halleonard.com

CONTENTS

ALL ABOUT THAT BASS

Flute

Words and Music by KEVIN KADISH
and MEGHAN TRAINOR

AMAZED

Flute

Words and Music by MARV GREEN,
CHRIS LINDSEY and AIMEE MAYO

ALL OF ME

Flute

Words and Music by JOHN STEPHENS
and TOBY GAD

APOLOGIZE

FLUTE

Words and Music by
RYAN TEDDER

BEAUTIFUL

FLUTE

Words and Music by
LINDA PERRY

BAD DAY

FLUTE

Words and Music by
DANIEL POWTER

D.S. al Coda

BAD ROMANCE

FLUTE

Words and Music by STEFANI GERMANOTTA
and NADIR KHAYAT

BEAUTIFUL DAY

FLUTE

Words by BONO
Music by U2

BEAUTIFUL IN MY EYES

FLUTE

Words and Music by
JOSHUA KADISON

BECAUSE I LOVE YOU
(The Postman Song)

FLUTE

Words and Music by
WARREN BROOKS

BELIEVE

Flute

Words and Music by BRIAN HIGGINS,
STUART McLENNEN, PAUL BARRY,
STEPHEN TORCH, MATT GRAY
and TIM POWELL

BUTTERFLY KISSES

FLUTE

Words and Music by BOB CARLISLE
and RANDY THOMAS

BRAVE

FLUTE

Words and Music by SARA BAREILLES
and JACK ANTONOFF

BREAKAWAY

from THE PRINCESS DIARIES 2: ROYAL ENGAGEMENT

Flute

Words and Music by BRIDGET BENENATE,
AVRIL LAVIGNE and MATTHEW GERRARD

BREATHE

FLUTE

Words and Music by HOLLY LAMAR
and STEPHANIE BENTLEY

CALL ME MAYBE

FLUTE

Words and Music by CARLY RAE JEPSEN,
JOSHUA RAMSAY and TAVISH CROWE

CANDLE IN THE WIND 1997

FLUTE

Words and Music by ELTON JOHN
and BERNIE TAUPIN

CHANGE THE WORLD

featured on the Motion Picture Soundtrack PHENOMENON

Flute

Words and Music by WAYNE KIRKPATRICK,
GORDON KENNEDY and TOMMY SIMS

CHASING CARS

FLUTE

Words and Music by GARY LIGHTBODY,
TOM SIMPSON, PAUL WILSON,
JONATHAN QUINN and NATHAN CONNOLLY

THE CLIMB
from HANNAH MONTANA: THE MOVIE

FLUTE

Words and Music by JESSI ALEXANDER
and JON MABE

CLOCKS

FLUTE

Words and Music by GUY BERRYMAN,
JON BUCKLAND, WILL CHAMPION
and CHRIS MARTIN

DON'T KNOW WHY

Flute

Words and Music by
JESSE HARRIS

COUNTDOWN

Flute

Words and Music by BEYONCÉ KNOWLES,
CAINON LAMB, JULIE FROST, MICHAEL BIVINS,
ESTHER DEAN, TERIUS NASH, SHEA TAYLOR,
NATHAN MORRIS and WANYA MORRIS

2nd time, D.C. al Coda

CODA

CRUISE

flute

Words and Music by CHASE RICE,
TYLER HUBBARD, BRIAN KELLEY,
JOEY MOI and JESSE RICE

CRYIN'

Flute

Words and Music by STEVEN TYLER,
JOE PERRY and TAYLOR RHODES

Moderately slow, in 2

DIE A HAPPY MAN

Flute

Words and Music by THOMAS RHETT,
JOE SPARGUR and SEAN DOUGLAS

DILEMMA

FLUTE

Words and Music by CORNELL HAYNES,
ANTWON MAKER, KENNETH GAMBLE
and BUNNY SIGLER

Moderately slow, in 2

Fine

2nd time, D.S. al Fine

DRIFT AWAY

flute

Words and Music by
MENTOR WILLIAMS

FIELDS OF GOLD

FLUTE

Music and Lyrics by
STING

DROPS OF JUPITER
(Tell Me)

Words and Music by PAT MONAHAN,
JAMES STAFFORD, ROBERT HOTCHKISS,
CHARLES COLIN and SCOTT UNDERWOOD

Flute

FALLIN'

FLUTE

Words and Music by
ALICIA KEYS

FIREWORK

Flute

Words and Music by KATY PERRY,
MIKKEL ERIKSEN, TOR ERIK HERMANSEN,
ESTHER DEAN and SANDY WILHELM

FOOLISH GAMES

FLUTE

Words and Music by
JEWEL KILCHER

FOREVER AND FOR ALWAYS

Flute

Words and Music by SHANIA TWAIN
and R.J. LANGE

FRIENDS IN LOW PLACES

Flute

Words and Music by DeWAYNE BLACKWELL
and EARL BUD LEE

FROM A DISTANCE

Flute

Words and Music by
JULIE GOLD

GENIE IN A BOTTLE

Words and Music by STEVE KIPNER,
DAVID FRANK and PAMELA SHEYNE

Flute

GET LUCKY

FLUTE

Words and Music by THOMAS BANGALTER,
GUY MANUEL HOMEM CHRISTO, NILE RODGERS
and PHARRELL WILLIAMS

HOW TO SAVE A LIFE

FLUTE

Words and Music by JOSEPH KING
and ISAAC SLADE

HELLO

Flute

Words and Music by ADELE ADKINS
and GREG KURSTIN

Moderately slow

HERE AND NOW

Flute

Words and Music by TERRY STEELE
and DAVID ELLIOT

HERO

Flute

Words and Music by ENRIQUE IGLESIAS,
PAUL BARRY and MARK TAYLOR

HEY, SOUL SISTER

Flute

Words and Music by PAT MONAHAN,
ESPEN LIND and AMUND BJORKLUND

HO HEY

FLUTE

Words and Music by JEREMY FRAITES
and WESLEY SCHULTZ

Moderately slow, in 2

HOLD ON, WE'RE GOING HOME

Flute

Words and Music by AUBREY GRAHAM,
PAUL JEFFERIES, NOAH SHEBIB,
JORDAN ULLMAN and MAJID AL-MASKATI

HOME

FLUTE

Words and Music by GREG HOLDEN
and DREW PEARSON

Moderately, in 2

THE HOUSE THAT BUILT ME

Flute

Words and Music by TOM DOUGLAS
and ALLEN SHAMBLIN

HOW AM I SUPPOSED TO LIVE WITHOUT YOU

Flute

Words and Music by MICHAEL BOLTON
and DOUG JAMES

I FINALLY FOUND SOMEONE

from THE MIRROR HAS TWO FACES

Flute

Words and Music by BARBRA STREISAND,
MARVIN HAMLISCH, R.J. LANGE
and BRYAN ADAMS

Moderately slow

I GOTTA FEELING

Flute

Words and Music by WILL ADAMS,
ALLAN PINEDA, JAIME GOMEZ,
STACY FERGUSON, DAVID GUETTA
and FREDERIC RIESTERER

I KISSED A GIRL

Flute

Words and Music by KATY PERRY,
CATHY DENNIS, MAX MARTIN
and LUKASZ GOTTWALD

I SWEAR

FLUTE

Words and Music by FRANK MYERS
and GARY BAKER

I WILL REMEMBER YOU

Theme from THE BROTHERS McMULLEN

Flute

Words and Music by SARAH McLACHLAN,
SEAMUS EGAN and DAVE MERENDA

JAR OF HEARTS

FLUTE

Words and Music by BARRETT YERETSIAN,
CHRISTINA PERRI and DREW LAWRENCE

JUST THE WAY YOU ARE

Flute

Words and Music by BRUNO MARS,
ARI LEVINE, PHILIP LAWRENCE,
KHARI CAIN and KHALIL WALTON

Moderately

LIPS OF AN ANGEL

Flute

Words and Music by AUSTIN WINKLER,
ROSS HANSON, LLOYD GARVEY, MARK KING,
MICHAEL RODDEN and BRIAN HOWES

LITTLE TALKS

FLUTE

Words and Music by
OF MONSTERS AND MEN

LET IT GO

FLUTE

Words and Music by JAMES BAY
and PAUL BARRY

NEED YOU NOW

Flute

Words and Music by HILLARY SCOTT,
CHARLES KELLEY, DAVE HAYWOOD
and JOSH KEAR

LOSING MY RELIGION

Flute

Words and Music by WILLIAM BERRY,
PETER BUCK, MICHAEL MILLS
and MICHAEL STIPE

Moderately fast

LOVE SONG

FLUTE

Words and Music by
SARA BAREILLES

LOVE STORY

FLUTE

Words and Music by
TAYLOR SWIFT

MORE THAN WORDS

Flute

Words and Music by NUNO BETTENCOURT
and GARY CHERONE

105

NO ONE

FLUTE

Words and Music by ALICIA KEYS,
KERRY BROTHERS, JR. and GEORGE HARRY

100 YEARS

FLUTE

Words and Music by
JOHN ONDRASIK

Moderately fast

REHAB

FLUTE

Words and Music by
AMY WINEHOUSE

THE POWER OF LOVE

Flute

Words by MARY SUSAN APPLEGATE
and JENNIFER RUSH
Music by CANDY DEROUGE
and GUNTHER MENDE

Slowly

ROAR

FLUTE

Words and Music by KATY PERRY,
LUKASZ GOTTWALD, MAX MARTIN,
BONNIE McKEE and HENRY WALTER

ROLLING IN THE DEEP

Flute

Words and Music by ADELE ADKINS
and PAUL EPWORTH

ROYALS

FLUTE

Words and Music by ELLA YELICH-O'CONNOR
and JOEL LITTLE

SAVE THE BEST FOR LAST

Flute

Words and Music by WENDY WALDMAN,
PHIL GALDSTON and JON LIND

SAY SOMETHING

Flute

Words and Music by IAN AXEL,
CHAD VACCARINO and MIKE CAMPBELL

Very slowly, in 4

SHAKE IT OFF

Flute

Words and Music by TAYLOR SWIFT,
MAX MARTIN and SHELLBACK

SECRETS

FLUTE

Words and Music by
RYAN TEDDER

Moderately slow, in 2

SHE WILL BE LOVED

Flute

Words and Music by ADAM LEVINE
and JAMES VALENTINE

SMELLS LIKE TEEN SPIRIT

FLUTE

Words and Music by KURT COBAIN,
KRIST NOVOSELIC and DAVE GROHL

SOMETHING TO TALK ABOUT
(Let's Give Them Something to Talk About)

FLUTE

Words and Music by
SHIRLEY EIKHARD

STAY WITH ME

FLUTE

Words and Music by SAM SMITH,
JAMES NAPIER, WILLIAM EDWARD PHILLIPS,
TOM PETTY and JEFF LYNNE

STACY'S MOM

FLUTE

Words and Music by CHRIS COLLINGWOOD
and ADAM SCHLESINGER

Medium Rock

STAY

FLUTE

Words and Music by MIKKY EKKO
and JUSTIN PARKER

Moderately

STRONGER
(What Doesn't Kill You)

FLUTE

Words and Music by GREG KURSTIN,
JORGEN ELOFSSON, DAVID GAMSON
and ALEXANDRA TAMPOSI

TEARS IN HEAVEN

FLUTE

Words and Music by ERIC CLAPTON
and WILL JENNINGS

TEENAGE DREAM

Flute

Words and Music by KATY PERRY,
BONNIE McKEE, LUKASZ GOTTWALD,
MAX MARTIN and BENJAMIN LEVIN

THINKING OUT LOUD

Flute

Words and Music by ED SHEERAN
and AMY WADGE

THIS LOVE

FLUTE

Words and Music by ADAM LEVINE
and JESSE CARMICHAEL

A THOUSAND YEARS

from the Summit Entertainment film THE TWILIGHT SAGE: BREAKING DAWN - PART 1

Flute

Words and Music by DAVID HODGES
and CHRISTINA PERRI

TILL THE WORLD ENDS

FLUTE

Words and Music by LUKASZ GOTTWALD,
MAX MARTIN, KESHA SEBERT
and ALEXANDER KRONLUND

Moderately fast

UPTOWN FUNK

Flute

Words and Music by MARK RONSON,
BRUNO MARS, PHILIP LAWRENCE, JEFF BHASKER, DEVON GALLASPY,
NICHOLAUS WILLIAMS, LONNIE SIMMONS, RONNIE WILSON,
CHARLES WILSON, RUDOLPH TAYLOR and ROBERT WILSON

VIVA LA VIDA

FLUTE

Words and Music by GUY BERRYMAN,
JON BUCKLAND, WILL CHAMPION
and CHRIS MARTIN

WAITING ON THE WORLD TO CHANGE

FLUTE

Words and Music by
JOHN MAYER

WE CAN'T STOP

Flute

Words and Music by MILEY CYRUS,
THERON THOMAS, TIMOTHY THOMAS,
MICHAEL WILLIAMS, PIERRE SLAUGHTER,
DOUGLAS DAVIS and RICKY WALTERS

Moderately slow

WE BELONG TOGETHER

Flute

Words and Music by MARIAH CAREY,
JERMAINE DUPRI, MANUEL SEAL, JOHNTA AUSTIN,
DARNELL BRISTOL, KENNETH EDMONDS, SIDNEY JOHNSON,
PATRICK MOTEN, BOBBY WOMACK and SANDRA SULLY

Slow Soul

WE FOUND LOVE

Flute

Words and Music by
CALVIN HARRIS

WHAT MAKES YOU BEAUTIFUL

Flute

Words and Music by SAVAN KOTECHA,
RAMI YACOUB and CARL FALK

WHEN YOU SAY NOTHING AT ALL

Flute

Words and Music by DON SCHLITZ
and PAUL OVERSTREET

YOU RAISE ME UP

FLUTE

Words and Music by BRENDAN GRAHAM
and ROLF LOVLAND

YEAH!

Flute

Words and Music by JAMES PHILLIPS,
LA MARQUIS JEFFERSON, CHRISTOPHER BRIDGES,
JONATHAN SMITH and SEAN GARRETT

YOU WERE MEANT FOR ME

Flute

Words and Music by JEWEL MURRAY
and STEVE POLTZ

YOU'RE BEAUTIFUL

FLUTE

Words and Music by JAMES BLUNT,
SACHA SKARBEK and AMANDA GHOST

Moderately slow

YOU'RE STILL THE ONE

Flute

Words and Music by SHANIA TWAIN
and R.J. LANGE

YOU'VE GOT A FRIEND IN ME

from Walt Disney's TOY STORY

Flute

Music and Lyrics by
RANDY NEWMAN

101 SONGS

BIG COLLECTIONS OF FAVORITE SONGS ARRANGED FOR SOLO INSTRUMENTALISTS.

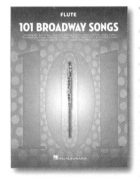

101 BROADWAY SONGS

00154199	Flute	$14.99
00154200	Clarinet	$14.99
00154201	Alto Sax	$14.99
00154202	Tenor Sax	$14.99
00154203	Trumpet	$14.99
00154204	Horn	$14.99
00154205	Trombone	$14.99
00154206	Violin	$14.99
00154207	Viola	$14.99
00154208	Cello	$14.99

101 HIT SONGS

00194561	Flute	$16.99
00197182	Clarinet	$16.99
00197183	Alto Sax	$16.99
00197184	Tenor Sax	$16.99
00197185	Trumpet	$16.99
00197186	Horn	$16.99
00197187	Trombone	$16.99
00197188	Violin	$16.99
00197189	Viola	$16.99
00197190	Cello	$16.99

101 CHRISTMAS SONGS

00278637	Flute	$14.99
00278638	Clarinet	$14.99
00278639	Alto Sax	$14.99
00278640	Tenor Sax	$14.99
00278641	Trumpet	$14.99
00278642	Horn	$14.99
00278643	Trombone	$14.99
00278644	Violin	$14.99
00278645	Viola	$14.99
00278646	Cello	$14.99

101 JAZZ SONGS

00146363	Flute	$14.99
00146364	Clarinet	$14.99
00146366	Alto Sax	$14.99
00146367	Tenor Sax	$14.99
00146368	Trumpet	$14.99
00146369	Horn	$14.99
00146370	Trombone	$14.99
00146371	Violin	$14.99
00146372	Viola	$14.99
00146373	Cello	$14.99

101 CLASSICAL THEMES

00155315	Flute	$14.99
00155317	Clarinet	$14.99
00155318	Alto Sax	$14.99
00155319	Tenor Sax	$14.99
00155320	Trumpet	$14.99
00155321	Horn	$14.99
00155322	Trombone	$14.99
00155323	Violin	$14.99
00155324	Viola	$14.99
00155325	Cello	$14.99

101 MOVIE HITS

00158087	Flute	$14.99
00158088	Clarinet	$14.99
00158089	Alto Sax	$14.99
00158090	Tenor Sax	$14.99
00158091	Trumpet	$14.99
00158092	Horn	$14.99
00158093	Trombone	$14.99
00158094	Violin	$14.99
00158095	Viola	$14.99
00158096	Cello	$14.99

101 DISNEY SONGS

00244104	Flute	$16.99
00244106	Clarinet	$16.99
00244107	Alto Sax	$16.99
00244108	Tenor Sax	$16.99
00244109	Trumpet	$16.99
00244112	Horn	$16.99
00244120	Trombone	$16.99
00244121	Violin	$16.99
00244125	Viola	$16.99
00244126	Cello	$16.99

101 POPULAR SONGS

00224722	Flute	$16.99
00224723	Clarinet	$16.99
00224724	Alto Sax	$16.99
00224725	Tenor Sax	$16.99
00224726	Trumpet	$16.99
00224727	Horn	$16.99
00224728	Trombone	$16.99
00224729	Violin	$16.99
00224730	Viola	$16.99
00224731	Cello	$16.99

HAL•LEONARD®
www.halleonard.com

Prices, contents and availability subject to change without notice.

0718